How to create

Amazing

tantalizing Book

cover for

FREE

Tips, tricks for Self-Publishing Book

ISBN: **1496147561**
ISBN-13: **978-1496147561**

1. Professional looking Book Cover for FREE
    a. Conceptualize the concept
    b. Be prepared
    c. Have everything you need
    d. Program's to be used
2. Basic knowledge, inserting text and more
    a. Create fancy background
    b. Text, choices and placing
    c. Background options
3. Images give it a professional look
    a. Attention grabbing flare.
    b. What image can be used?
    c. Finding images
    d. Rules in picking images
    e. Remove background of an image
4. Editing keeps the critics at bay
    a. Editing images
    b. Clean finish
    c. Steps I normally take
5. Sources for more tips & tricks

How to create Amazing tantalizing Book cover for FREE
tips, tricks for Self-Publishing Book

As the saying goes "You can't judge a book by its cover", but the reality is: a run-of-the-mill, unpolished unprofessional looking book cover can keep potential buyers and readers at bay or moving to the next suggested book on Amazon's extensive list.

Let's face it, there are three things that directly influence the sale of any book at first glance, of which are: price, title and book cover appearance. The reality is that online book sales depend on these three factors. Yes, being a well-known popular author is a plus – but many authors selling books online today are simply not. For the beginning author, or even if you have self-published several books on Amazon, Barns & Noble or on Google play, self-published authors have a hard time getting sales when competing with the finished glossy amazingly interesting book cover that sits just above or below their book listing.

Yes – price is and can be a defining factor. Most people search for books and they filter their search just like you and I probably do; from low to highest price. I know very few people who do not search for books online in this manner – but as a self-publishing beginner author, the book price usually is low because few people know the author and the best way to get people to try out a new book written by an unfamiliar author is to start off with the lowest possible price that the author is comfortable with.

The second factor which is the title depends on the author and to some degree the genre that the author is writing for. Science fiction and thrillers do well with fancy interesting titles – on the other hand technical books or self-help books normally do not. With that said, picking the right title for a book is sometimes a hit or miss kind of thing. Since this book focuses on creating a stunning eye catching book cover, I will simply leave the book title up to you to decide.

The third factor is the book's cover image. Now this, this can be a sales killer or a deal maker. On several occasions I have found myself looking at certain books simply because I was intrigued by the appearance of the book cover in cooperation with the title – this is not to say that I purchased the book. However, it did move me to read more about the book, to explore the books preview sample and ultimately to have interest in the book itself.

The Book cover image, tied together with the help of price and title will draw potential customers in to investigate, to read more about the book, where they can then be "moved" to purchase your book. Obviously I am not saying a great book cover will insure a sale – you need a good description, a few good reviews, and most of all wonderful amazing book content.

What I am simply saying is: a bland, unprofessional looking book cover can directly influence how people will react to your book listing on any online book store.

So ultimately the desire of any author is to sell books; the goal is to create a carefully well written book filled with wonderful content, followed by creating an inviting attention-grabbing professional looking cover that works in collaboration with the proper title and price. If you can accomplish this, your chances of selling more books greatly increase.

Professional looking Book Cover for FREE

So how do you get an amazing professional polished book cover image?

You can pay $300 or more for a good looking book cover or you can try to find a college student with publishing knowledge that will create it for you on the "cheap" (just remember one thing: you get what you pay for). Or like many self-publishing authors have done; you can create a wonderful looking cover to match that superbly written book or novel.

Now this is not to say that you cannot write a book that has a so-so non-traditional unprofessional unpolished cover and not make it big. Just look at Harry Potter and the Philosopher's Stone, have you seen the original cover of J.K. Rowling's first book? In fact, once the 'Harry Potter' books made it big the publishers that signed up to publish the books later on made several changes to the original cover.

So the question is: What author writes a book that he or she does not want people to read? Or what author does not want to make money in order to sustain his or her lifestyle – like being able to eat and pay the rent?

When I wrote my first book, "for Children How to Become Rich Successful and Do well in school", I decided that I wanted to create my own book cover. For me, money was not the issue – it was simply a desire to be part of the entire book making process. Looking back now – I wish I had paid the money for a clean professional interesting book cover. The cover I created was nice, clean but simple. I did enjoy the knowledge I gained as I underwent the process to create the cover, but it was clearly obvious for all to see that this was not a professionally produced cover.

Several months later I came back to my book and realized that I could do better, that I can create a wonderful enticing professional book cover image and that I can do it for free.

After creating my new book cover I presented it to several honest reviewers and some harsh critics, of which gave it many a glowing praises. Even with this accomplishment I found myself at a crossroad. My book had sold several copies, my marketing endeavors such as flyers, book marks, online presence had already been assimilated; the old book cover image had become a staple of all my online presence. My fear was that if I changed the already familiar book cover at such a late stage I may not be able to change all of my marketing efforts, of which proliferated the internet and drives traffic to my book. This late date change would clash and even possibly hinder all my marketing efforts.

So my suggestion to you is to create the perfect cover for your book now.

As I wrote this book I took several trips through Amazon's book listings. I did numerous searches for several different types of books and I noticed one important thing; there were quite a few if not an exceedingly amount of book covers that were basic generic copies of each other. I mean there were books that the only difference between them was the title and the name of the author.

During some searches (especially those that were free or priced below $1.99) the covers were exactly the same bland simple background – there was nothing that stood out and said: "hey look at me!" I am sure that you have noticed it before, but the point I want to make is that instinctively I was dubiously repulsed by the covers. The impression it gave me was that if the author could not find the time to make an interesting, clean polished book cover image, what does that say about the content of the author's book?

This is why I quickly changed my mind about my marketing dilemma and I replaced my first books cover image. It was my book, it represents me as the author and I did not want people taking their first look at my book cover and thinking, "if this is the best he can do for the cover, he probably didn't put forth much effort into his content as well."

As I mentioned before – a great book cover does not sell books, wonderfully written content does, but how will they "desire" to read the content of the book if the cover screams bland, boring, unpolished and unprofessional?

Let us begin: please remember that this is written in order to teach, to instruct and not to entertain.

Step 1: Plan out design of cover.

Before getting into the low tech method of creating the book cover, let me mention one thing.

This book does not go into detail about "how" to come up with the idea or the ideas for your book cover. I do not know what your book is about or the overall message you want to convey with your book cover – you are the author; only you at this stage of self-publishing know what your book is about and how to best translate that message to your book cover image.

You as the author, clearly understanding what your book is about, should already have a preconceived vision, an idea for the look of your book cover. The process of creativity starts with a simple idea – think of how and what you want your cover to look like, the message you desire to depict by means of the cover and put it on paper. It does not have to be an extravagant piece of art work, all you need to start with is a simple sketch, at minimum, in order to help you have a mental image of what you want the finished product to look like.

How it will look, the placing of the words and any images to be used in or incorporated into the book cover should be carefully thought out beforehand.

The worst thing you can do is to start creating a cover image without a preconceived idea. While a blank canvas to a seasoned artist may be an open invitation in to the world of the imagination, to the average person it is simply a blank space of nothingness offering no direction or worse – too many choices of incoherent ideas.

A few steps to follow:

- **Conceptualize the concept.** Sometimes coming up with the "concept" can be easy or it can be extremely difficult. I find that the easiest way to come up with an idea that you can put into words or in an image is by simply playing with the concept of the book itself. Depending on what you are writing about, the story, the plot, the genre, the idea for the cover may simply just pop into your head. Other times it may be just a vague fuzzy image that is stuck in the back of your brain that you can barely grasp at.

From time to time all you need in order to come up with an amazing book cover image idea is to simply think about the highlight of the story, just like music a story has a crescendo, a climax, a moment in the book or a message that encapsulates one of the most important things (substance, plot, concept or idea) in your book. Try to capture that in your book cover image.

- **Be prepared.** First create the idea, a starting point. How do I want the cover to look like and does it fit well with the overall content of the book? Personally I have been drawing cartoon images for a very long time and in my youth I took a home study course on art, sketching and painting. This experience has helped me easily come up with my book cover ideas on the preverbal fly as one might say. But if you lack the artistic background don't worry, all you have to do is take a little bit of time researching other book covers and it will come to you. So as part of the "first step" all you really need to do, is to come up with a basic sketch that you can put on paper, an idea, a concept of the desired finished product, nothing major, just something that will help you stay focused.

- **Have everything you need at hand.** When you have come up with an idea, when you have decided on the concept of your book cover – before you start, find everything you need beforehand and have it ready to use. Have all of the images or different designs picked out and ready to use. Every font you found interesting, an image or even a background color; have it on file, stored safely and ready to use. This also goes for any programs you may need to use.

Waiting to get images or fonts while you are knee deep in the development stage of creating your book cover will simply bog down the whole process and can easily create confusion. There should be a set plan in motion; everything you need should be saved, set up and easily available to you. I suggest that backup copies should always be made of images. I have had many a horrible experiences where a difficult to find image was lost or horribly altered and it took me weeks to find it again.

Remember: Start with a fixed idea, changes can be added later on but only after you have already accomplished your first draft design.

- **Program's to be used.** The most important program necessary to accomplish your goal is Microsoft's PowerPoint presentation program, the next program needed is MS Paint and an image editing program is required (I personally use Irfanview – it is a free image editing program found online that can be easily downloaded and is extremely easy to use).

I am hoping that you are fairly comfortable and somewhat knowledgeable in the use of MS PowerPoint and MS Paint. If not, do not worry I will try to give as much detail as I possibly can to insure that you will be able to effortlessly create a book cover image. But I do suggest that if you are not familiar with how to use the many, many functions provided by the MS PP (power point) program, follow the links provided to you at the end of this book (of which all are free resources).

Basic knowledge, inserting text and more

Though you can be as creative as you want with your book title, book covers usually have little when it comes to text (words). Nevertheless I have seen book covers littered with a large amount of words (having extremely long Book title). Some have done this in order to stuff key words into their title in an attempt to help with possible SEO (search optimization) techniques. Of course this means that if you have a very long title, Amazon just like any other self-publishing service will require you to have your entire title on the book cover.

As I stated before – I am not here to tell you how to create, how to choose or to teach you how to brainstorm on how to come up with the title of your book. I will simply leave that up to you since you know best what you are writing about and how you want your title to reflect your body of work.

Now comes the tricky part – what do you want for the background?

Why do I mention the back ground now? I bring it up because depending on what kind of background you use, this will affect the look of the font. The color of the font may clash or simply blend and/or disappear into the background.

If you want an image as the background for the cover you have to consider what kind of image works best (this will be covered in the image portion) with your font text. Now if you plan on having a solid color or an interesting array of fading or blending colors all you need to worry about is the font type and font colors.

The basics of step 2 are simple and will be broken up into two parts:

Step 2.a: Create fancy colored basic background canvas.

Step 2.b: Adding text, choices and placing.

Step 2.a: Create fancy colored basic background canvas.

You have decided on having a solid, fancy, colored background as the backdrop to your cover and adding images is not in your current plan – that is ok, nothing wrong with that.

MS PowerPoint has a simple feature that gives you the ability not only to change the color of the background but it also gives you the capability of creating wonderful, interesting arrangements with the background colors.

For example, you can have one color fade into another. Creating a more complex arrangement of colors simply requires having several colors that fade into another color and you can easily change the placing of the fading as well. I would say that it is easy but "it is and it's not" – like my son likes to say.

I am currently using MS PowerPoint 2013, which can cause some confusion when I am describing where to go to find certain functions or tabs since older versions sometimes have these tab functions placed in other locations. But all in all once you have the general idea of how and what can be done finding a tab is easy once you get familiar with your MS PowerPoint version.

(* Trust me, I had a horrendous time trying to find some functions when I upgraded from MS PowerPoint 2007 to 2013.)

Background options

The easiest thing to do is to go to the "slide Orientation" tab (found at design tab) and to switch the PowerPoint orientation from landscape to portrait. This will help give you a better feel for the look of your cover – don't worry if it is not the right trim size that can be corrected later.

Now all you need to do is to right click on the slide to open the tool option box. The option you are looking for is "format background". This will open a new options box with several choices you can choose from. I would suggest that you learn a bit about all the options available to you, but for the purpose of this book I will only focus on two options.

Option one: Solid Fill

Option two: Gradient fill

Solid fill is fairly easy to use, what you are basically doing is choosing a solid color for the whole slide. You pick the color and your done – you can even adjust the transparency a bit as well. An option to make all available slides have the same background is given and personally, I always have at minimum two slides open. One is the one I keep and the other slide is for playing and trying out new things (insuring that if changes do not work my original is safe). So by all means, if you have more than one slide available choose this option.

As you can see due to MS PowerPoint's desire to make great presentations the colors are vibrate and of great quality – exactly what we need for the book cover.

If a solid color is not what you are going for you have the second option: Gradient fill.

Gradient fill is basically a tool that allows you to have two or more colors that bleed or blend into one another. If you noticed for the cover of this book I used an original bland book cover I had for one of my books sitting side by side with a new fancy more polished cover image. The new cover image had the "gradient fill" option used to blend two separate colors together. I also used some of the features available to make the picture of the calculator more dramatic as it fades into cover (I used the transparency feature for this effect).

This is where trial and error, and a whole lot of practice, will come into play. I say this because if I gave you a rundown of each feature provided by MS PowerPoint this eBook would be more than three hundred pages long – while full of technical help, it would be as boring as reading a dictionary on a cool Saturday afternoon (not happening). This is why I have provided links to free resources where you can, if you choose to do so, to get free technical detailed information on MS PowerPoint.

When you choose the gradient fill option, you will be presented with more options at the bottom portion of the box. You have a selection of colors to choose from, you are even provided with the use of a simple slide bar feature to move the colors as well as where they meet and blend together. You can even choose to have more than two colors if that is the look you are going for. My suggestion: if you are a beginner stick with the two colors design and learn how to manipulating this option well before moving on to the more difficult option with three or five colors.

(* A simple option may be to use the pre-prescribe layouts that come with the program. Some of these options can make an interesting background cover for any book. I am certain that you can even find for free or purchase layouts online. But like I said – I prefer free and learning how to do something on my own, is fun.)

Step 2.b: Adding Text, choices and placing

The wonderful thing about MS PowerPoint is the ease in which anyone can add text to the document slide. If you happen to be familiar with PowerPoint or not, it does not take much to learn how to insert a text box into a slide, you are given several choices of text, fonts and word art. The simple ease in which you can click on that little green dot and tilt the text to the exact position you want it to appear on the cover; I love it.

(A simple reminder) Before going on, the layout of the PowerPoint presentation should be changed from layout to portrait. Depending on what power point version you have, this option can easily be found in one of the above tabs, either in the home tab or its own design and/or layout tab. In either case find this option and change the panel to the portrait layout.

Text and Font

It's as simple as 1, 2, and 3. Choose from the options provided in the tabs above; decide on what type of font will be used for the text portion of the book or e-book cover. The Title of the Book should have already been decided upon and a desired look by now is established through the pre-staging or planning process. All that needs to be done is to use the text tools to make it come to life (it may take you some "playing" and "tweaking" with to make it look exactly as how you envisioned or desired, but take your time).

One of the best features, in my opinion, is the ability to move the text where ever you what on the slide. This comes in handy when trying to figure out the placing or spacing of the text you plan to use as your title for the cover. Originally I created my simple book covers with MS Paint, but one of the problems I faced was the inability to easily change, move or even rearrange the text on the cover – on MS Paint once the text box is closed, that was it no going back unless you erased the whole thing and started over.

With MS PowerPoint you do not have this problem, in fact you can even add effects to your text such as 3D, fading, change the size of the font and even when you close the text box, you can always go back and make changes without having to erase and start over.

All you have to do is click on the insert tab above and choose the word "art tab". You have two options, the plain text and the word art text. Personally I mostly use the word art text option, it gives you wonderful stunning font and color options to choose from.

Again, this will require some practice and a bit of trial and error to learn all of the possible features that can be used to make your text and cover look great.

The basic's in a nut shell is this: click on the word art tab and a text box opens up in the slide. Type in the desired phrase and then you can either alter the size, font, select the bold or italic options and if that is not enough, there is so much more that can be done. Simply right click the mouse in the text box and a pop up box will appear with several options. You can format the text, use the 3D feature and the list simply goes on and on.

Helpful tip with Text

On occasion you may have text that overlaps on two separate colors, whether separated by a defined lined contrast or blends from one color to another. This may cause the text, depending on the color used to possibly blend or appear to fade.

A simple but effective way to fix this would be to use the format text glow effect provided by MS PowerPoint.

This depends on the Windows version you are using: You need to select the text box you are working with. Right click on the text box and a pop up window with options opens. Click on the "Glow & Soft edges" option, this gives you several options to choose from. Click on the color dropdown. Select the color that fits your needs, for instance if you have text that sits on a black background for the top portion and a soft tan color for the below portion and the text is white – choose the black glow effect to encircle the text in a 'black glow' allowing the text to pop. There is also a Shadow button which simplifies things a lot at the cost of a loss of fine control.

In essence, all I can say is that you will have several selections to choose from to create the perfect polished book cover to compliment the wonderful content of the book.

The next step is adding images – again, this is not necessary, but as you can see in my book cover it truly does help the overall look.

Images give it a professional look

"A picture is worth a thousand words"

The phrase refers to the notion that a complex idea can be conveyed with just a single still image. It also aptly characterizes one of the main goals of visualization, namely making it possible to absorb large amounts of data quickly. In the case of a single book cover it says, "I'm interesting and well worth reading!"

There have been many a time where I was awestruck by a single image; on screen, a simple photo or by a well-designed advertisement. A single image can and does say much. In the case of the self-publishing author it can say professionally polished and worth reading. It can also say amateurish and not worth the effort to read.

As I have stated before – a book can sell thousands of copies if it has great content and a growing fan base of readers. But nonetheless, a new or a not so well known author runs the risk of having his work ignored if the cover does a poor job of attracting the attention and the eye of potential readers. With this in mind we move toward our next step in the creative process.

Step 3: Images added for attention grabbing flare.

As noted above, an image can be used to covey the feel, the content or the excitement of the subject matter inside the book. While images do not have to be used, sometimes it may be just what the doctor ordered.

So when and if deemed necessary you should consider also adding to the cover interesting images (as a solid background or as an accent compliment to the cover image), depending on the overall look. It would be helpful to remember not to overwhelm the appearance of the book cover. The desire should be to create excitement and interest, but also an easy to read cover. What I am saying is the person looking at the cover should easily understand the message your book cover wants to convey.

(* If you choose to have the background as a picture or an image, this can be done by following the same steps used in the instructions given in formatting the background color – simply use the picture or texture fill option.)

Adding images can be done by simply using the insert function of MS PowerPoint to insert images easily into the slide.

Please remember that images inserted into the PowerPoint slide can be moved, tilted, formatted and even altered with the artistic effect option. Let us not forget the ability to alter the image as well. You can position an image any way you want, give it a 3D look and even remove the background of an image inserted into the slide (some images like "PNG" do not work well with this function).

What image can be used?

Images can be taken by you of a live scene, taken by a professional photographer or purchased online by one of several online photo sources – it all depends on which way you choose to go. Just remember that if you purchased an image online you need the right to use the image for commercial use and some sources have limits. You can pay for a subscription in order to use an image found on their site, but there may be unforeseen added expenses or extra charges. Several sites may have restrictions on how many times a photo stock can be downloaded or reprinted.

The rights to images are a bit of a legal minefield. If you use your own images and people appear in them, you are expected to have written permission to use said people for the commercial use of the image. The same is true of certain buildings and works of art. This is one man's understanding of a complex subject in which he is not an expert. A quick Google search will help you find more on this issue.

(* If creating your own image from several images, images should be saved and formatted in the GIF form in order to utilize the transparency feature in the image editing program or in the MS PowerPoint program.

The steps I normally use are as followed. I create an image, save it in PNG format for best quality and then I use IrfanView to crop, sharpen image, I also increase the DPI of image to 300 or 400 and then I save it in the format best suited for my use.)

Finding and choosing the right pictures

The quality of your book cover will mostly depend on what pictures or art you use, and how well they fit together, so in this section I'm going to outline where you can find royalty free images, and basic rules to use when choosing images or pictures for your book cover.

Here are some sites that are used most often: for stock pictures or images

123rf.com

Bigstockphotos.com

Depositphotos.com

Photodune.net

Shutterstock.com

Dreamstime.com

iStockphoto.com

Side note: The problem with using stock pictures is that if it looks good enough to use, someone has probably already used it as well – this can take away from the uniqueness of a cover which defeats the whole purpose of creating an interesting amazing book cover.

The RULES for picking photos:

1) Simple is better

2) Needs to cause an immediate emotional reaction

3) Not too busy or too many colors

4) Don't use a GREAT picture, use the overlooked one

5) Blend and match colors

One of the advantages I have is that I started creating book covers and other works of arts by using MS Paint. This knowledge and experience has allowed me some added flexibility by knowing how to somewhat alter pictures in a way that will help me make even a familiar image seem unique. I have used MS Paint to merge pictures and to alter images. I even once was able to use MS Paint transparent feature to merge my daughters picture with a picture of one of her favorite movie stars, at the time she was 8, and it simply blew her away. That is what a great book cover image should do, excite, intrigue, and if possible blow the costumers mind away.

Now this is not to say that this cannot be done with one of the amazing Adobe products, but remember, I was looking for inexpensive and easy to use methods. I tried learning how to use Adobe to alter images and between figuring out the program, getting flustered by not grasping how to use the flat or other features of the program, I simply gave up.

By all means if you have a copy of Adobe and you have experience using the program, I am not saying that you cannot use it to create an amazing book cover. What I am saying is, use everything that you have at your disposal to create the best book cover image that you possibly can.

I am confident in my belief that if you are creative enough to write wonderfully intriguing content for your book, you also have the creative ability to envision an even more stunning book cover that conveys the message you want to make.

Help tip: remove the background of image

How to add or combine two or more different images and have the background removed from the image in a PowerPoint slide, a slide with a colored background?

There is a quick and easy fix to get rid of the background, be it a solid color or not, of an image, as long as that image is either formatted as a GIF or a PNG file format.

1. Select the insert picture tab from the ribbon.
2. Locate the desired image which has been saved on your computer and insert it into the slide. This will activate the picture tools toolbar on the ribbon.
3. Once the image has been added to the slide, click on the image to select it, if it is not still selected.

Note - If you have clicked on another tab on the ribbon since you have added the image, when you select the image again, the picture tools toolbar may not be shown. Simply click on Format, directly above the ribbon. The Picture Tools toolbar will appear once again.

1. PowerPoint 2013
   a. Insert GIF or PNG image.

b. Click 'remove background' tab.

c. PowerPoint attempts to determine which part of your image is the subject of the picture. The background is then displayed in purple.

   In addition to this, a special 'Background Removal' tab will appear on the Ribbon. Mark the sections you desire to remove as well as the sections you may desire to keep.

   (*) It takes a bit of practice but it's a great tool.

2. PowerPoint 2010

   a. On the left side of the ribbon, click on the Color button

   b. At the bottom of all the selections, click on the set transparent color tab. Your mouse pointer will change to the transparency tool.

(*) You can also use 'remove background' tab.

3. PowerPoint 2007
    a. On the left side of the ribbon, select Recolor > Set Transparent Color. Your mouse pointer will change to the transparency tool.
    b. Click on the background color of the image, the color you wish to remove.
    c. The background color of the image disappears.

IMPORTANT: The goal of this book is to help you create the best professional looking book cover image possible in an easy inexpensive manner that will not consume all of your time trying to learn how to do it or in achieving it. You are an author and you should be spending most of your time doing

what authors are meant to be doing, writing
great works of art.

Editing keeps the critics at bay

"I don't even like showing my stuff to publishers and editors much."
~ Christopher Hitchens

Personally I hate editing; I can never truly know if I am doing more harm than good. Every time I check for mistakes, alterations or simply to insure that my work fits what I have envisioned I want to make changes. Being sort of a perfectionist when it comes to art is a flaw I try to hide, but when it comes to writing, I need all the help in the world. I am sort of the straight to the point kind of person and usually what I envision in my mind is not what I am clearly capable of conveying on paper. To this end I have editors, critics and the harshest of these critics is my wife and daughter.

Editing is important – though lately, I have found errors in many great books – but nevertheless, the pictures, the images, the finished product of your book cover will always need some editing. It is simply that important.

Step 4: Editing images & knowledge.

This is where a bit of editing knowledge will come in handy with creating the amazing, tantalizing book cover you desire.

I am saddened to say, editing is something that is required through the whole book cover creative process. You start with an idea and you share that idea with a few honest critics to see if the idea conveys the message you desire. You then put a simple plan together, get your font types, image or images together – you figure out the setup of the layout and you make a mockup of the cover. Then you boldly present it to the critics again and this will usually mean you will need some alterations, changes and some touch up.

To be honest, each picture (if more than one is used) will require some form of editing so trust me when I say that after you have created your first amazing book cover, you will simply find the next cover image (in basic terms) easier to do.

By the time you succeed with a book cover that your critics will love and you are happily satisfied with, you will still need to complete some simple editing necessary to complete your work.

Clean finish and minor changes.

Once you've accomplish the look you want for your book cover, you can clean up the image as a whole or make minor changes to improve the finished look of the cover. Try to avoid making too many changes and be smart – create a copy and only alter the copy so if an error occurs, nothing is lost.

The steps that I normally take are:

1. After coming up with the image I want for the book cover in MS PowerPoint, I click on the full screen view (like if I was presenting the slide). This will give me a perfect view of how the cover will feel and look.

2. I then use a wonderful feature called the "print screen" option, some people call it a screen shot. This will copy the entire screen, an exact replica.

3. I then open MS Paint and paste the image onto the blank canvas.

* This will often give you a large image that cannot be completely seen; simply use the view button option to zoom out in order to help see the entire image on the screen.

4. Then I merely use the "cut" feature to select and capture the book cover only; I paste this in a new MS Paint canvas. Make sure there are no borders or missing sections of the image that are needed.

5. Save the file as a PNG formatted file to save the quality of the image.

6. Open IrfanView or your preferred image editor program and open the file there.

7. In the editing program you can do a bit more cropping, sharpen the color and any other small changes you

might deem appropriately necessary to the image.

8. Then change the DPI of the image to 300 or 400. This may not matter much for a digital eBook cover but for a print cover this will protect the quality of the image and will help reduce any distortion of the image when changing the size of the image.

9. For print books: depending on the size of your book, change the size of the image to the appropriate size. This will also insure that the image looks more like a book cover (until now the size as in width may have kept it from looking as such).

   Important: remember to 'uncheck' the box in your image editor when resizing image that preserves the aspect ratio of an image.

* I follow this step even for my eBooks because it gives it the book shape appearance I desire and I want nothing left to chance – every little bit of "professional" aspect helps my book shine when it is sitting on a very long list of competing Amazon books.

10. Save file using the PNG format and then save a second copy in whatever format your self-publishing company requires you to use for uploading.

In the end, all this work will culminate with you having an amazing wonderfully completely polished and professionally looking book cover image that will help potential buyers take not only a first but a second and closer look at your book.

(* I also save the MS Power Point I was working on to create the cover with separate copies of any and all the images I used. This will insure that if I ever need to make changes to the cover image in the future, it can be easily done with no fuss or muss.)

Remember that a good book cover image doesn't sell books, it takes much more than that; a good description, author bio, good reviews and most important of all, great enjoyable or informative book content.

* * * * *

Words from the Author

Please, if you found this book to be helpful and informative, stop by Amazon and leave a favorable review. Thank you.

I would like to thank you for reading my Book and I hope that it was beneficial to your needs.

Please feel free to look up and read some of my other books:

For children how to become Rich Successful & do well in school

Written to motivate children and inspire them to love learning: much of the book is filled with tips and ideas that I use with my two straight 'A' honor students.

**You are worth millions
you just don't know it**

Young people today have lost sight of their worth and their wealth. They have an opportunity to make their life a success, but without the right tools or the right frame of mind most young people will cast aside their one in a lifetime opportunity. This book will teach them some very important lessons in order to him them reach a better and more successful life.

Author: William Medina
Title: How to create Amazing tantalizing Book cover for FREE, tips, tricks for Self-Publishing Book

Again, I thank you.

Next page: Sources for basic & advanced.

Sources for more basic and advanced tips, tricks and help

To learn more beneficial "tips and Tricks" to using Microsoft Power Point more efficiently and creatively please follow the links below to some very helpful online resources.

- Microsoft PowerPoint Slide Effects - Example slide effects with instructions http://office.microsoft.com/en-us/templates/results.aspx?ctags=CT0103 36615

- **University of Wisconsin-Eau Claire** http://www.uwec.edu/Help/office/powe rpoint-win2010.htm

- **Florida Gulf Coast University** http://www.fgcu.edu/support/office200 7/ppt/index.asp
- **Indezine PowerPoint Tutorials** http://www.indezine.com/products/pow erpoint/learn/

Free PowerPoint Templates

- **Templates from the PowerPoint team**
  http://blogs.office.com/b/microsoft-powerpoint/archive/2011/01/17/fabulou s-free-templates-await-the-ppt65-project-is-complete.aspx

- **Templates from the Rapid E-Learning Blog** http://www.articulate.com/rapid-elearning/5-free-powerpoint-e-learning-templates/

- **Free templates & downloads from the E-Learning Heroes community**
  http://community.articulate.com/downl oads/

- **Microsoft PowerPoint Templetes**
  http://office.microsoft.com/en-us/templates/CT010117272.aspx

FAQs

- **PowerPoint for Macintosh- Getting Started**
  http://www.microsoft.com/mac/powerp

oint/getting-started-with-powerpoint

- **PowerPoint for Windows - Getting Started**
  http://office.microsoft.com/en-us/powerpoint-help/basic-tasks-in-powerpoint-2010-HA101824346.aspx